Green Lantern

SECRET ORIGIN

SECRET ORIGIN

Geoff Johns
Writer

Ivan Reis
Penciller

Oclair Albert
Inker

Randy Mayor
Colorist

Rob Leigh
Letterer

With
Julio Ferreira Partial Inker Book 3
Ivan Reis Partial Inker Book 6

Original Series Covers by
Ivan Reis and **Dave McCaig**

Eddie Berganza Editor-original series
Adam Schlagman Associate Editor-original series
Bob Harras Group Editor-Collected Editions
Sean Mackiewicz Editor
Robbin Brosterman Design Director-Books

DC COMICS
Diane Nelson President
Dan DiDio and Jim Lee Co-Publishers
Geoff Johns Chief Creative Officer
Patrick Caldon EVP-Finance and Administration
John Rood EVP-Sales, Marketing and Business Development
Amy Genkins SVP-Business and Legal Affairs
Steve Rotterdam SVP-Sales and Marketing
John Cunningham VP-Marketing
Terri Cunningham VP-Managing Editor
Alison Gill VP-Manufacturing
David Hyde VP-Publicity
Sue Pohja VP-Book Trade Sales
Alysse Soll VP-Advertising and Custom Publishing
Bob Wayne VP-Sales
Mark Chiarello Art Director

**GREEN LANTERN: SECRET ORIGIN
(NEW EDITION)**

DC Comics, 1700 Broadway, New York, NY 10019
A Warner Bros. Entertainment Company
Printed by Dubuque, IA, USA. 3/2/11. First printing.

ISBN: 978-1-4012-3086-9

INTRODUCTION BY **RYAN REYNOLDS**

I was never an expert on Hal Jordan. I'd always known the gist of the character: I knew he wore a lot of green. Had a ring possessed of infinite power bestowed upon him by a dying alien. And I knew he's survived many successors and wildly diverse iterations over an astonishing multi-decade run. If you like sports analogies, he's the New York Yankees. Lately though, I've gotten to know the guy pretty damn well. Like Hal Jordan, I too was given the gift of a ring. Mine was more symbolic in its power but no less auspicious. I was asked to put that ring on and bring Hal Jordan to life in a whole new form: Film. Not a job I take lightly.

About a year and a half ago, I first sat down with Martin Campbell, Donald DeLine, and a man whom I consider responsible for the resurgent interest in Green Lantern, Geoff Johns. They were all eager to build a big screen superhero who would both live up to his lengthy legacy, yet simultaneously find a foothold with a whole new audience – young and old alike. Hal Jordan was about to become a living, breathing person. And I was going to be the guy to do it. No pressure…

True fans of Hal Jordan know the caliber of hero we're talking about. From the moment I came aboard, I saw the challenge and opportunity in creating a classic yet modern day hero who can throw a punch, tell a joke and kiss the girl. I saw the guy as a cross between Chuck Yeager and Han Solo. The Green Lantern saga is so limitless in its scope, I'm sure it was a relief for the writers to know it was going to be an origin story of sorts. They need look no further than the starting point.

Green Lantern encompasses a seemingly limitless supply of adventure: fighter jets, space travel, action, aliens, betrayal, humor, tragedy, heroes, villains, and even a rather complicated little love story. These are just a few ingredients which have been a part of this epic for over 50 years.

It's a great time to be a superhero fan. Technology is such that bringing Green Lantern to life properly is finally possible. Creating energy constructs based upon infinite will and pure imagination can vividly appear before our very eyes. This technological leap also happened to coincide with a time period in which the world is fascinated by big screen comic book adaptations.

Preparing to get Hal up and running in living color was helped greatly by this book, SECRET ORIGIN, illustrated beautifully by Ivan Reis who I had the pleasure of meeting on the set in New Orleans. This book basically gave me the introduction I was looking for in order to begin the incredible ascent to Oa. I hope you like it.

Actor **Ryan Reynolds** stars as Hal Jordan in the upcoming Green Lantern movie.

"WHAT ARE YOU AFRAID OF?"

PEOPLE LIKE TO ASK ME THAT. WHEN THEY DO, THEY HAVE THIS KNOWING GRIN ON THEIR FACES. AS IF THEY EXPECT ME TO ANSWER, "NOTHING."

I HUMOR THEM MOST OF THE TIME, BECAUSE THAT'S WHAT THEY WANT ME TO SAY.

"I'M NOT AFRAID OF ANYTHING."

THEY THINK I WAS BORN WITHOUT FEAR.

THEY'RE WRONG.

THEY THINK THIS RING GIVES ME THE POWER TO DO ANYTHING.

THEY'RE WRONG ABOUT THAT TOO.

BEFORE I WAS GIVEN THE GREATEST WEAPON IN THE UNIVERSE, BEFORE I JOURNEYED TO THE STARS--

--MY DAD GAVE ME THE POWER TO DO ANYTHING.

HE TOLD ME I COULD BE WHATEVER I WANTED TO BE.

DAMMIT. I'M HAVING SOME *PROBLEMS* HERE, FERRIS. OIL'S GETTIN' EATEN UP *QUICK*. I THINK THE LAST OF MY TORQUE PINS JUST *FAILED*.

I THOUGHT THIS WAS SENT TO I-LEVEL REPAIR.

IT *WAS*.

DADDY!

DADDY, THAT BOY IS BREAKING THE *RULES*!

ONE MINUTE, HONEY, OKAY?

I NEED TO BRING IT IN. *AWAY* FROM THE CROWD.

THERE'S NO EXTERNAL LEAKAGE. THE INVESTORS ARE *WATCHING*.

THAT'S *FIFTEEN-MILLION DOLLARS* AND OUR LAST *SIX YEARS* OF *DEVELOPMENT* YOU HAVE IN THE *AIR*.

KEEP IT *FLYING*, JORDAN.

THIS THING'S GOING *DOWN*, FERRIS.

ON TOP OF YOU, COAST CITY, OR RIGHT HERE...

...AND RIGHT *HERE* NO ONE ELSE GETS *HURT*.

WHEN YOUR WORST FEAR HAPPENS IN FRONT OF YOUR EYES--

DAD.

--I THOUGHT THERE WAS NOTHING *LEFT* TO BE AFRAID OF.

MOM THOUGHT THERE WAS EVERYTHING.

I'M SO *SORRY,* KEN.

IT'S OKAY, JESSICA...

...HE'S JUST GOT A LOT OF HIS FATHER IN HIM.

HOW MANY *TIMES* HAVE YOU *PROMISED* ME YOU WOULDN'T GO TO THE AIRFIELDS, HAL?

YOU SAID *FERRIS AIR.*

YOU ARE NOT ALLOWED *ANYWHERE* NEAR A PLANE, DO YOU UNDERSTAND ME, YOUNG MAN?

DO YOU?

YES, MA'AM.

I DIDN'T *UNDERSTAND* HER.

AND SHE DIDN'T *UNDERSTAND ME.*

NO ONE DID.

NICE GOING, *JERK.*

SHUT *UP,* JACK.

MOM WAS *FREAKING OUT* WHEN MR. ARDEN CALLED. SHE ALMOST HAD A HEART ATTACK!

OW.

YOU SCARE MOM LIKE THAT AGAIN AND THERE'S PLENTY MORE.

DON'T FIGHT! DON'T FIGHT!

WE'RE *NOT,* JIM.

WE AREN'T MOVING.

BUCKLE UP.

BETTER SAFE THAN SORRY. MOM SAYS SO.

BUCKLE UP.

BEFORE MOM HAS TO TELL YOU TO.

KLIK

SON?

CAN I HELP YOU?

I'M EIGHTEEN TODAY, SIR.

BOOOOMM

MAJOR JONATHAN "HERC" STONE. HE FLEW WITH MY FATHER, CARL FERRIS AND KEN ARDEN. THEY WERE KNOWN AS THE *FOUR MUSKETEERS.*

STONE WAS THE ONLY ONE WHO CONTINUED HIS CAREER IN THE USAF. HE EARNED SO MANY SILVER STARS HE OUTNUMBERED THE AMERICAN FLAG.

HE DIDN'T LIKE ME VERY MUCH.

HE'S APPROACHING *MACH THREE,* MAJOR.

MACH *THREE?!*

MACH *THREE.*

THREE POINT ONE.

HAHA *HAAA!* I'VE GOT HER *REALLY* KICKING NOW!

DAMMIT, HIGHBALL, WE'RE TESTING STRUCTURAL LIMITATIONS AT MACH *ONE,* SHE'S NOT READY TO--

GIVE HER SOME *CREDIT,* MAJOR! SHE'S STILL HOLDING AT MACH THREE POINT *TWO!*

MACH THREE POINT *THR--!*

RRRRRMMMMBBBBLLLL

TNKK -TNKK TNKK

HEY, STONE...

YOU SEE THAT, STEWART? THAT *JET JOCKEY* JUST KNOCKED DOWN ONE OF *OURS.*

HERE WE GO.

HERE WE GO.

HEN IT COMES TO WAR, WE MIGHT ALL BE ON HE SAME SIDE. BUT IF YOU THINK THERE'S NO TERSERVICE RIVALRY BETWEEN THE MERICAN ARMED FORCES--

--YOU'RE AS SHARP AS A JARHEAD.

YOU SHOULD BE *HAPPY.*

THIS IS MORE *FIGHTING* THAN THE AIR FORCE WILL SHOW YOU ALL YEAR.

THEN I BETTER MAKE IT *COUNT.*

HAL?

JIM?

IT'S PAST *TWO* IN THE MORNING. WHAT ARE YOU DOING--?

I KNOW THIS IS YOUR HANGOUT. I'VE BEEN WAITING FOR YOU. LIKE ALWAYS.

BRO, I--

MOM'S DYING.

WHAT IS IT?

CANCER. IT STARTED IN THE PANCREAS. AND IT'S *BAD.*

I NEED TO SEE HER.

YOU *CAN'T.*

WHAT DO YOU MEAN I CAN'T?

YOU KNOW WHAT MOM SAID. AS LONG AS YOU'RE IN THE AIR FORCE--

THIS IS *DIFFERENT,* JIM.

THE DOCTORS SAID THE STATE SHE'S IN, ANYTHING *UPSETTING* COULD TRIGGER ALL SORTS OF *PHYSICAL* PROBLEMS.

JACK WON'T LET YOU.

I CAN'T LET YOU EITHER.

THE NEXT MORNING, I GOT TO BASE EARLY. INSTEAD OF REPORTING RIGHT TO STONE'S OFFICE, I TOOK AN UNAUTHORIZED JOYRIDE.

IT WAS THE FIRST TIME I DIDN'T SMILE IN THE AIR.

WHEN I LANDED, STONE WAS WAITING FOR ME.

...THE LAST TIME THE AIR FORCE LOST THIS MANY JETS IN *ONE WEEK* WE WERE AT WAR IN VIETNAM.

NOW I'VE GOT TO CALL THE PENTAGON AND EXPLAIN HOW WE LOST A THIRTY MILLION DOLLAR FIGHTER ON A DAMN *TEST FLIGHT* TO DETERMINE...

..."STRUCTURAL LIMITATIONS OF THE F-16 AT MACH ONE." THIS WASN'T EVEN A *COMBAT* SIMULATION!

YOU MAY BE THE "*BEST*" PILOT ON *PAPER*, BUT IN *REALITY* YOU'RE THE MOST *EXPENSIVE* AND THE *MOST DANGEROUS*.

IT'S TIME YOU USE THAT *LUMP* ON YOUR SHOULDERS ONCE IN AWHILE.

STONE'S WORDS WERE JUST A FOG AROUND ME. LIKE JACK'S.

BUT I ALWAYS LISTENED TO JIM. AND THAT'S ALL I WAS HEARING.

"MOM'S DYING."

I JUST TOOK HER FOR A SPIN, MAJOR.

WITHOUT CLEARANCE AND WITHOUT AUTHORIZATION, JOYRIDING LIKE IT WAS YOUR *LAST* FLIGHT.

IT WAS. I KNEW IT WAS.

I COULDN'T SAY IT. I COULDN'T WALK AWAY. I COULDN'T QUIT.

I HAD TO FIND ANOTHER WAY OUT.

ANOTHER BAD CHOICE IN A LIFE FULL OF THEM.

HAL? HOW DID YOU...?

I CAME TO SEE MOM. YOU CAN TELL HER I WAS DISCHARGED, JIM. I'M *OUT* OF THE AIR FORCE.

YOU CAN TELL HER I KEPT MY PROMISE.

HAL, THERE WAS A COMPLICATION THIS AFTERNOON...

...MOM'S GONE.

WHAT? WHAT HAPPENED?

YOU KILLED HER.

JACK?

AFTER YOU *RAN AWAY*, SHE SPENT HER *LIFE* WORRYING.

SHE *HEARD* ABOUT ALL THE *CLOSE CALLS*. ALL THE *CRASHES*.

YOU KILLED MOM!

JACK! THIS IS TOUGH FOR *ALL* OF US--

SINCE WHEN IS *ANYTHING* TOUGH FOR HAL, JIM? WHEN DAD DIED *I* TOOK CARE OF MOM. I GOT A JOB TO HELP.

WHEN HAL RAN AWAY I LEFT COLLEGE. I MOVED HOME.

I GAVE MY *LIFE* FOR OUR FAMILY JUST LIKE MOM.

I WAS DAD'S SON. JIM WAS MOM'S. JACK WAS ALWAYS ON HIS OWN PATH...

WHEN HAS HAL *EVER* GIVEN THIS FAMILY *ANYTHING?*

...BUT I TOOK HIM OFF IT.

I WAS NEVER A GOOD BROTHER TO ANYONE.

NOK NOK

JIM? COME ON IN--

I CAN'T.

SUSAN'S WAITING IN THE CAR.

SOMETHING I WISH I COULD'VE GIVEN YOU A *LONG* TIME AGO.

WHAT'S *THIS*?

I THOUGHT NO ONE UNDERSTOOD ME.

I WAS WRONG.

TO MY BROTHER HAL

I'D BEEN DISHONORABLY DISCHARGED. I TORE MY FAMILY APART.

I STARED AT THAT PICTURE OF ME AND DAD ALL NIGHT. WONDERING...

...WHERE THE HELL DO I GO FROM HERE?

THERE IS NO ESCAPE.

YOU KNOW THAT, DON'T YOU, ABIN SUR? YOU BELIEVE OUR PROPHECIES.

THAT IS WHY I HAVE RETURNED TO THIS FESTERING PIT OF A PLANET, QULL. I CAN HEAR THE SADISTIC LAUGHTER YOU DEMONS SHARE OVER THE HORROR THAT APPROACHES OTHERS.

I WILL STOP THAT HORROR. I WANT TO KNOW MORE ABOUT THE PROPHECIES YOU HAVE SEEN.

QUIET, QULL! YOU HAVE TOLD ABIN SUR ENOUGH!

THOSE SECRETS REMAIN WITH US, GREEN LANTERN!

I HAVE HAD ENOUGH, ATROCITUS!

YOU DO NOT GET TO CHOOSE WHEN YOU TALK TO ME AND WHEN YOU DO NOT.

AAARRG!

I WILL KNOW EVERYTHING YOU KNOW, DEMONS. ABOUT THE FATE OF THE UNIVERSE. ABOUT COSMIC REVELATIONS.

AND ABOUT "THE BLACKEST NIGHT."

ACCORDING TO THE PROPHECY, EARTH IS THE *BIRTHPLACE* OF THE *BLACK*. THE *ANTITHESIS* OF THE *EMOTIONAL SPECTRUM*.

THE *EMPTINESS* THAT IS SAID TO *ONE DAY* CONSUME *ALL* LIGHT AND *ALL* LIFE.

"THE *BLACKEST NIGHT*" AGAIN, ABIN?

I AM *INCREASINGLY* WORRIED ABOUT YOU, MY FRIEND. YOU HAVE BECOME *OBSESSED* WITH THESE *LIES*.

AND NOW YOU FLY USING A *SHIP* RATHER THAN RELYING ON YOUR *RING*.

IT HAS BEEN *FORETOLD* MY RING WILL *FAIL* ME WHEN I MOST NEED IT.

"FORETOLD" BY THE PRISONERS OF THE PLANET YSMAULT. THOSE *DEMONS* WEAVE THEIR TALES IN AN ATTEMPT TO INSTILL *FEAR* INTO YOUR HEART AND THE *GREEN LANTERN CORPS*.

ALTHOUGH THE *GUARDIANS FORBID* FURTHER DISCUSSION, I WILL FIND *PROOF* OF THIS INEVITABLE *RISE* OF *DARKNESS*.

ATROCITUS WILL LEAD ME TO THE PLACE THAT WILL GIVE *BIRTH* TO THE *BLACK*.

I WILL ONLY LEAD YOU TO YOUR *DEATH*, GREEN LANTERN!

ATROCITUS IS IN YOUR *CUSTODY*? YOU FREED HIM FROM HIS *CRUCIFIX* ON YSMAULT? THE GUARDIANS WILL HAVE YOUR RING IF THEY DISCOVER THIS.

WISH ME *LUCK* THEN.

...ABIN...EVEN IF I AM *WARY* OF THE VALIDITY OF ANY OF THIS, YOU DO KNOW IF YOU FIND SOMETHING AND IF YOU NEED BACKUP...

...NOT EVEN THE GUARDIAN'S *TERRITORIAL EDICT* WILL KEEP ME OUT OF YOUR SECTOR.

THANK YOU, *SINESTRO*.

ABIN SUR-- GREEN LANTERN OF SPACE SECTOR 2814--

--OUT.

I WAS CAPTAIN HAL JORDAN.

NOW I WAS JUST HAL JORDAN.

DON'T LET LAMINSKI GET TO YOU, HAL.

...HAL? WHAT'RE YOU STARIN' AT?

THAT PLANE.

YEAH. TRASH HEAP'S SEEN BETTER DAYS. NOT GOOD FOR ANYTHIN' BUT PARTS.

I REMEMBER IT.

YOU REMEMBER IT?

MY DAD FLEW FOR A LOT OF AIRFIELDS IN COAST CITY. HE TOOK ME UP WITH HIM IN THAT PLANE ONCE.

LONG TIME AGO.

"DAD. I'M SCARED."

DON'T WORRY. YOU'RE FLYING WITH ME, SON.

YOU'VE NEVER FLOWN WITH ME.

I NEED TO GET BACK IN THE AIR.

I HAVE THE FINAL PAPERS. MY FATHER WOULD HAVE BROUGHT THEM HIMSELF, BUT APPARENTLY HE'S GOLFING THE GAME OF HIS *LIFE* IN PEBBLE BEACH.

IT'S *NICE* HE CAN ENJOY HIS GOLDEN YEARS.

CAROL. THIS IS HAL--

JORDAN. OF COURSE. IT'S BEEN A LONG TIME.

CAROL'S FATHER RETIRED A FEW YEARS AGO. SHE'S COME OUT OF THE COCKPIT TO RUN FERRIS AIR.

YOU'RE A PILOT?

I *WAS.* I HAVE MORE IMPORTANT THINGS TO DO.

LIKE *NOW*, MR. JORDAN.

HE'S A PROBLEM.

THE DEAL WAS YOU KEEP HIM ON.

MY FATHER'S NOT GOING TO LIKE THIS.

DAMMIT, DAD.

...AND I FEEL FREEDOM!

THE IRONY OF IT ALL. IN THE MOMENT OF DEATH, YOUR RING DID NOT FAIL YOU, LANTERN.

YOU FAILED IT.

KRNNMM

N-NO.

AAARRR!

FREEDOM!

GOODBYE, GREEN LANTERN.

YOU HAVE NOT LEAPT TO FREEDOM. YOU HAVE ONLY LEAPT TO YOUR *DEATH*. RING. WHAT IS THE SHIP'S PROJECTED POINT OF *IMPACT*?

DOWNTOWN COAST CITY, CALIFORNIA. LOSS OF LIFE ESTIMATED AT TWENTY-TWO HUNDRED AND TEN TERRESTRIALS.

THEN I CANNOT ABANDON THIS SHIP. I HAVE TO...FORCE A LANDING SOMEWHERE ELSE.

K'AA-TANGG

BOOOOMMM

‑KAFF‑

...RING. PREPARE MESSAGE AND FILE INFORMATION FOR SINESTRO. HE MUST CONTINUE MY MISSION. IT IS NOT ONE FOR A ROOKIE...NNN...

SPACE SECTOR SCAN 2814 FOR REPLACEMENT SENTIENT INITIATED.

HAL JORDAN.

WHAT--?

YOU HAVE BEEN CHOSEN.

BOOOMMMM

I AM ABIN SUR. GREEN LANTERN OF YOUR SPACE SECTOR.

SPACE SECTOR 2814.

I AM DYING.

THE BRIGHTEST DAY BECOMES THE BLACKEST NIGHT.

TO SERVE IS A GREAT HONOR.

BESTOWED UPON YOU BY THE RING.

THE RING IS FUELED BY YOUR WILLPOWER.

THE GREATEST POWER IN THE UNIVERSE.

A UNIVERSE WHERE EVIL IS CONFRONTED BY THE GREEN LANTERN CORPS.

BY THE ORDER OF THE GUARDIANS.

THE RING WILL MAKE YOUR THOUGHTS AND WISHES A REALITY.

THE GREEN LANTERN'S LIGHT MUST BE RECHARGED WITH THE POWER BATTERY.

BUT THERE IS A FLAW IN THE BATTERY, AN IMPURITY LOCATED WITHIN YOUR VISUAL SPECTRUM.

THE POWER IS INEFFECTUAL AGAINST YELLOW.

YOU HAVE BEEN CHOSEN FOR ONE REASON.

AMONG MANY OTHERS.

YOU ARE A MAN WHO CAN OVERCOME GREAT FEAR.

HAL JORDAN OF EARTH.

WHAT--?

GREEN LIGHT GRAFTED OVER MY BODY. IT WAS HOT.

FWOOOSHH

BUT THE BLACK WAS AS COLD AS ICE.

I NEED SOME AIR. GOTTA GET OUT.

WILLPOWER RECOGNIZED. RING ONLINE.

WHO IS THAT? WHO'S TALK--?

ORDERS ACCEPTED.

IS THAT THE RING?

AFFIRMATIVE.

BOOMMM

HOLY #?$%!

HOLY #?$%!

HOLY #?$%!

THERE WAS NO RUMBLING OF ANY ENGINE.

NO STICK TO PULL ON.

NO TOWER TO GET PERMISSION FROM.

IT WAS JUST ME.

ME AND THE RING.

BOOOOMM

HAHAHA HAAA!

...YOU ARE CLEAR TO OPEN ENGINE FOUR, LAMINSKI.

LAMINSKI? DO YOU COPY?

YEAH, YEAH. I COPY THAT, TOWER.

YOU HEARD THE NEWS, RIGHT? FERRIS AIR BOUGHT ARDEN OUT. CARL FERRIS--

CARL FERRIS HAS BEEN RETIRED FOR YEARS. HE'S GOT THAT SWEET LITTLE PIECE OF MEAT HE CALLS A *DAUGHTER* RUNNING HIS AIRFIELDS.

WITHIN A WEEK, I'LL BE TEACHIN' HER A NEW MEANING FOR THE TERM "LANDING STRIP--"

LAMINSKI? LAMINSKI, WHAT THE HELL WAS THAT?

I... I DON'T...

TEN TIMES THE PILOT.

YOU'RE LOSING CONTROL! LAMINSKI?!

LOSE YOUR COOL AT FIFTEEN THOUSAND FEET--

--PAY THE PRICE. C'MON, LAMINSKI.

STEADY.

STEADY NOW.

WHAT THE HELL HAPPENED, TOM?

I SAW SOMETHING GLOWING, MR. ARDEN. SOMETHING *GREEN.*

OW.

SENTIENTS APPROACHING.

CONCEALING IDENTITY.

Hnn.

STOP *DOING* THAT.

WHOA.

Um. HI.

YOUR PILOT MIGHT, *uh*, NEED SOME MEDICAL ATTENTION. I THINK I HEARD HIM THROW UP.

WHO THE HECK ARE YOU?

GREEN LANTERN OF SPACE SECTOR 2814.

GREEN... LANTERN?

WHAT'S A "GREEN LANTERN"?

KLUK

I'M CURIOUS WHAT A "GREEN LANTERN" IS *MYSELF,* CAROL.

I ASKED THE SAME QUESTIONS EVERYONE AT FERRIS DID.

ABOUT THIS ALIEN.

HE WAS OBVIOUSLY SOME KIND OF SOLDIER OR OFFICER.

I WASN'T GOING TO LEAVE HIM OUT IN THE OPEN.

HE DESERVED BETTER THAN THAT.

NO MATTER WHO HE WAS.

THE GREEN LANTERN? IS THAT WHAT *THIS* IS?

RING? RING, YOU CAN *TALK* NOW.

THIS IS YOUR POWER BATTERY.

POWER BATTERY? WHAT'S A POWER BATTER--

HEY!

A GREEN LANTERN'S POWER BATTERY IS THEIR POWER RING'S CHARGING STATION. RECHARGING REQUIRED APPROXIMATELY EVERY TWENTY-FOUR TERRESTRIAL HOURS.

LET GO, DAMMIT!

INCORRECT OATH.

KLANK

POWER LEVELS 100%.

GREEN LANTERN OF SPACE SECTOR 2814.

YOU WILL REPORT TO OA FOR TRAINING IMMEDIATELY.

WHAT?

HAVE A NICE FLIGHT.

WHERE THE *HELL* AM I?

THE PLANET OA. CENTRAL PRECINCT OF THE GREEN LANTERN CORPS.

AND HOME TO THE GUARDIANS OF THE UNIVERSE-- IMMORTAL WATCHERS AND PROTECTORS OF ALL.

ABIN?

DISENGAGING AUTOPILOT.

WAIT. WHY DID YOU BRING ME HERE?

WHAT AM I SUPPOSED TO DO NOW?

HELLO?!

TUTORIAL OFF.

SSSAATTT

IS THAT A *HUMAN?*

A *HUMAN* GREEN LANTERN?

WHAT'S A HUMAN?

HA HA HA HA HA HA HA HA

THAT'S NO WAY TA TREAT YOUR *BATTERY.*

NICE LANDIN', POOZER.

NAME'S KILOWOG.

WELCOME TA RINGSLINGIN' 101. OR AS KE'HAAN AND I LIKE TO CALL IT--

--THE WORST DAY A' YOUR WORTHLESS LIFE!

OH, I GET IT.

THIS IS BOOT CAMP.

GET IN LINE WITH THE REST OF THE WHITE CIRCLES.

SHOOOM

IT'S WHERE YOU PRIMORDIAL QUADRUPEDS BELONG.

YOU WANNA BOX?

LET'S BOX.

SPLATTT

YOU REALLY SHOULDN'T HAVE DONE THAT.

WHY NOT?

BECAUSE I'VE BEEN LOOKIN' ALL DAY FOR SOMEBODY TA MAKE AN EXAMPLE OUTTA!

THEY WERE TRACKING IT WHEN IT FLEW PAST MARS.

BUT IT WASN'T UNTIL IT *TURNED* TOWARD EARTH THAT IT WAS RED FLAGGED.

SOMETHING BROKE OFF WHEN IT ENTERED THE ATMOSPHERE. RIGHT ABOVE BIG BEAR, CALIFORNIA.

FORT ROCK'S SENT A UNIT TO INVESTIGATE THE SECOND CRASH SITE. WE'RE HANDLING THIS ONE.

WHAT IS IT, MAJOR STONE? A FALLEN SPY SATELLITE? A METEOR?

YOU'RE THE SCIENTIST THAT SPECIALIZES IN THE THEORETICAL, DR. HAMMOND.

YOU TELL US.

MY GOD...

"...WE'RE NOT ALONE."

SOMETHING LANDED HERE.

LOOKS LIKE IT SLID INTO THE WATER.

WE MIGHT NEED SOME S.E.A.L.S TO...HEY.

YOU GUYS SEE THAT? THE WATER'S BOILING.

BLIP

RRAAAARRRR!

DEATH WILL CLAIM YOU. YOU AND ALL THAT THE GREEN LANTERN CORPS RULE OVER.

SO SWEAR THE SURVIVORS OF SECTOR 666.

THE RING CAN MAKE WHATEVER **TOOL** YA NEED. JUST GOTTA PICTURE IT IN YOUR MIND. **WILL** IT TO **LIFE**.

FORCE FIELDS. ENERGY BEAMS.

EVERYONE SEE THAT?

YES, **SIR**.

YOU PRACTICE **WELL**, AHTIER. WHY DO YOU SPEAK SO **LITTLE**?

BECAUSE I **FEAR** MY **DUTY**, KE'HAAN.

GREEN LANTERNS BURN **BRIGHT**, BUT THEY BURN OUT **QUICKLY**.

IF THAT **HUMAN** CAN MAKE IT, SO CAN **YOU**.

THANKS FOR THE RIDE, BUT I'LL GET OFF HERE.

K'RSHH

YOU **WILLED** YOURSELF FREE, EARTHMAN...

...NOW TRY CATCHIN' *THIS*.

NnNGg

WHAT THE HELL HAPPENED?

WHAT DO YOU MEAN WHAT HAPPENED, HUMAN? IT WAS *YELLOW*.

EVERYONE IN THE UNIVERSE KNOWS A GREEN LANTERN'S POWER RING IS *INEFFECTUAL* AGAINST *YELLOW*.

HE DON'T KNOW NOTHIN' 'BOUT THE CORPS, CH'P. HE'S FROM *EARTH.*

ASK ME, KILOWOG, EARTH'S A BACKWARD WORLD BEST LEFT TO THEIR *OWN.*

WHY *YELLOW?*

WHAT?

WHY WOULD THESE RINGS NOT BE ABLE TO AFFECT ANYTHING *YELLOW?*

YOU DON'T ASK QUESTIONS IN THE CORPS. YOU DO YOUR *DUTY.*

I DON'T EVEN KNOW WHAT THAT *"DUTY"* IS.

"TO SERVE AND PROTECT YOUR RESPECTIVE SECTORS AND ALL LIFE WITHIN THEM."

NOW DON'T GET ALL *PUFFY CHESTED* AGAIN. NEXT TIME, I WON'T BE SO NICE.

KILOWOG.

LET ME SPEAK WITH THE EARTHMAN.

WHAT BUSINESS IS HE OF YOURS, TOMAR?

HE'S WEARING *ABIN SUR'S* RING.

MY NAME IS *TOMAR-RE* OF XUDAR. GREEN LANTERN OF SPACE SECTOR 2815.

BY ALL ACCOUNTS, I AM YOUR *NEIGHBOR.*

I'M HAL JORDAN.

ABIN SUR'S REPLACEMENT IN THE CORPS. MY RING IS UNABLE TO *UNLOCK* HIS LOG...HOW DID HE DIE?

HE CRASHED HIS SHIP IN THE DESERT.

HIS *SHIP?*

HE DIDN'T *NEED* THAT SHIP.

THEN WHY WAS HE FLYING ONE?

HE DID WHAT NO GREEN LANTERN SHOULD. HE ALLOWED HIMSELF TO FEEL *FEAR.*

AND IT HAPPENED BECAUSE ABIN SUR DISOBEYED THE GUARDIAN'S TERRITORIAL EDICT AND PURSUED AN ENEMY *OUTSIDE* OF HIS SECTOR.

HE CAME INTO CONFLICT WITH A GROUP KNOWN AS THE EMPIRE OF TEARS.

AFTERWARD, HE GREW INCREASINGLY *PARANOID.*

HE BECAME *OBSESSED* WITH *DOOMSDAY PROPHECIES* AND *PRISMS.*

FRACTURED LIGHT. SPLINTERED SOULS. NOTHING MADE SENSE.

NOTHING MAKES SENSE TO ME RIGHT NOW.

THIS IS THE *BOOK* OF *OA*. IN IT-- TALES OF THE GREEN LANTERN CORPS.

ABIN SUR'S TALE IS NOW AMONG THEM. AN ENDING *TRAGIC*.

ONE DAY *YOUR* TALE WILL BE HERE TOO, AS WILL MINE.

A WORD OF ADVICE, SUCCESSOR.

IF YOU NEED HELP--

--ASK FOR IT.

THE SUN NEVER SET.

YER SUPPOSED TA FLY *AROUND* THEM, JORDAN, NOT *THROUGH* THEM!

I DIDN'T KNOW HOW LONG I GOT MY ASS HANDED TO ME.

I'LL DO IT.

YOU WON'T DO IT.

IT'S JUST A *COLOR.*

DAYS.

YOU MISHANDLE YOUR POWER BATTERY AGAIN, HAL JORDAN, AND SHORM WILL MISHANDLE *YOU.*

UNDERSTOOD, SALAAK.

YOU STILL GOT *CRACKS* IN YOUR CONSTRUCTS, JORDAN--

--BUT IT AIN'T BAD.

A WEEK?

YA DIDN'T DO IT *GRACEFULLY* AND YA DIDN'T DO IT *EASY*, BUT AS FAR AS I'M CONCERNED YER NOT COMPLETELY *USELESS*.

YOU *EARNED* YOUR *BADGES*.

SO LET'S LIGHT 'EM UP!

IN BRIGHTEST DAY IN BLACKEST NIGHT

IN BRIGHTEST DAY... IN BLACKEST NIGHT

NO EVIL SHALL ESCAPE MY SIGHT

NO EVIL SHALL ESCAPE MY SIGHT

LET THOSE WHO WORSHIP EVIL'S MIGHT...

LET THOSE WHO WORSHIP EVIL'S MIGHT

CLOSE THE DOOR!

WHAT IS IT?

THE SHIP'S FUEL ISN'T A *LIQUID!* IT'S POWERED BY SOME KIND OF *ROCK!*

LOOKS LIKE A METEOR.

GET HAMMOND CLEAR!

HE'S GOING INTO CONVULSIONS!

NnNNnnNn!

HAMMOND'S SO *CREEPY.*

WH-WHAT DID YOU SAY?

MEDIC! WE NEED A *MEDIC!*

LOOKS LIKE HE'S ALL RIGHT. TOO BAD.

GOD, I HOPE HE'S ALL RIGHT.

THAT MUSTACHE MAKES HIM LOOK LIKE A PEDOPHILE.

WHAT'S WRONG WITH HIS HEAD?

HECTOR HAMMOND IS A LOSER.

TERRIBLE TASTE IN SUITS.

HE'S ALWAYS CALLING CAROL FERRIS. LIKE SOME KIND OF STALKER.

SHUT UP.

HIS BREATH IS TERRIBLE.

CHARGING MY POWER ON AN ALIEN WORLD. [GRAD]UATING FROM AN [INTER]GALACTIC BOOT CAMP.

AS SOON AS I WAS DONE, I WAS COVERED IN GREEN LIGHT. I WAS TOLD MY RING WOULD ALERT ME TO ANY EXTRATERRESTRIAL INCIDENTS I SHOULD INTERVENE IN.

THEN I WAS SHIPPED BACK HOME.

HAL?

TOM?

I CAN'T BELIEVE IT! YOU'RE THE *GREEN LANTERN!*

ANY LIFE OUTSIDE THE CORPS WASN'T TAKEN INTO CONSIDERATION.

THE... GREEN LANTERN?

WHAT ARE YOU, *uh,* TALKING ABOUT?

WELL, YOU'RE WEARING A GLOWING GREEN *RING.*

AND THERE'S *THIS.*

WHAT DO YOU MEAN YOU'RE NOT A SUPER-HERO? YOU *CAUGHT* LAMINSKI'S PLANE LAST WEEK!

ANYONE ELSE WOULD'VE DONE THE SAME IF THEY *COULD.*

EVEN IF HE *IS* A JERK.

WELL, YOU'RE NOT GONNA HAVE TO WORRY ABOUT *HIM* ANYMORE.

I'M NOT SUPPOSED TO USE THE RING TO SORT OUT *PERSONAL PROBLEMS,* TOM.

NO, I MEAN THE *WALKOUT.*

WHAT WALKOUT?

KLANG

SEE ALL THE *EMPTY* LOCKERS?

ONCE WORD SPREAD THAT CAROL "LADY" FERRIS WAS TAKING THE REINS FROM MR. ARDEN, NO ONE WAS PARTICULARLY *EXCITED.*

AND AFTER HER FATHER DIDN'T SHOW FOR THE BIG *COMPANY SPEECH,* SHE HAD TO GIVE IT HERSELF--

--AFTERWARDS JUST ABOUT EVERYONE *QUIT.*

...OF COURSE, I'D MAKE IT WORTH YOUR TIME, MR. TRAINOR. PLENTY OF PAY AND BENEFITS AND A SHARE IN THE PROFITS...

...IF YOU KNOW OF ANY OTHER *PILOTS* THAT YOU'D LIKE FLYING ALONGSIDE YOU...

MY FATHER'S STILL TRAVELING. HE'LL BE OUT OF THE COUNTRY THE REST OF THE...

YES, OF COURSE, HE WOULD'VE MADE THE CALL HIMSELF IF HE COULD, BUT...

MR. TRAINOR, LISTEN TO ME. THIS IS THE OPPORTUNITY OF A... MR. TRAINOR?

...LARRY?

NOK NOK

YES?

MISS FERRIS.

MR. JORDAN? WHAT ARE YOU DOING HERE?

I JUST WANTED TO THROW IN MY RESIGNATION ALONG WITH THE REST.

YOU HAVEN'T SHOWN YOUR FACE HERE ALL *WEEK*. I ASSUMED YOU ALREADY HAD.

YOU ASSUMED RIGHT. I GUESS I WANTED TO MAKE IT *OFFICIAL*.

AND IF YOUR *FATHER* WAS HERE--

WHAT?

WHAT WOULD YOU *DO* IF MY FATHER *WAS* HERE?

I'D TELL HIM WHAT I'VE BEEN WANTING TO FOR *YEARS*.

I'D TELL HIM EVERYTHING MY MOTHER *BEGGED* ME *NOT* TO.

YOU KNOW WHAT, JORDAN? LET'S MAKE THIS DAY EVEN *BETTER* THAN IT *HAS* BEEN.

TELL *ME*.

YOUR FATHER PUT *MINE* IN A *DEATH TRAP!*

HE SAVED A FEW *BUCKS* AND HE SENT HIM OFF IN A PLANE THAT NEVER HAD A *CHANCE* AT *LANDING*.

AND NOW, WHILE *MY* DAD IS *ROTTING* IN THE *GROUND*, YOURS IS PLAYING *PUTT-PUTT* ON THE GULF OF THE MEXICO, DRINKING A MARGARITA AND PROBABLY SMOKING A CIGAR THAT COSTS MORE THAN WHAT I MAKE IN A DAY!

YOU DON'T MAKE *ANYTHING*, JORDAN. YOU JUST *QUIT*, REMEMBER?

NOW IS THAT *ALL* YOU'VE GOT TO *BARK* ABOUT?

FORGET IT, "LADY" FERRIS. I'LL SAVE THE REST FOR *HIM* WHEN HE'S *BACK* FROM HIS EXTENDED *HOLIDAY*.

DO YOU WANT TO FLY AGAIN?

WHAT?

DO YOU WANT TO FLY AGAIN?

YES.

BUT NOT *HERE*.

THEN *WHERE*?

WHO'S GOING TO HIRE YOU?

AFTER EVERYTHING YOU'VE DONE. *WHO'S* GOING TO TAKE THAT *RISK*?

I DIDN'T NEED A PLANE TO FLY ANYMORE.

THE RING MADE IT EASY.

THE RING MADE IT TOO EASY.

PLEASE, HAL.

I NEED A PILOT. AND YOU NEED A PLANE.

FOR A SPLIT SECOND, I DIDN'T SEE THE SHARK I THOUGHT SHE WAS. I SAW THE LITTLE GIRL I'D MET ALL THAT TIME AGO.

SHE CRIED LOUDER THAN I DID WHEN MY FATHER'S PLANE CRASHED.

SOMEHOW I'D FORGOTTEN THAT.

I OFFER SACRIFICE FOR THE *PROPHECIES* CONTAINED WITHIN THE *LIQUID* OF *LIFE.*

I ASK FOR THE *NAME* OF THE BEING THAT WILL *BIRTH* THE *BLACK.*

HEAR MY *CRIES,* TASTE THIS *FLESH* AND GRANT ME A *GLIMPSE* OF *TOMORROW.*

WITH BLOOD AND RAGE OF CRIMSON RED

RIPPED FROM A CORPSE SO FRESHLY DEAD

TOGETHER WITH OUR HELLISH HATE

WE'LL BURN YOU ALL, THAT IS YOUR FATE!

THIS BEING HOLDS THE POWER.

WILLIAM... HAND.

IT FELT GOOD TO FLY.

BUT IN THE BACK OF MY HEAD, I KNEW I WAS FLYING FOR THE WRONG PERSON.

I CONVINCED MYSELF I WAS ONLY STAYING UNTIL CARL FERRIS CAME BACK.

UNTIL I FINALLY GOT AN ANSWER TO THE QUESTION I'VE ASKED MYSELF A MILLION TIMES OVER.

HOW COULD HE LIVE THE WAY HE DOES AFTER WHAT HAPPENED?

HOW COULD HE SHIRK THE RESPONSIBILITY?

I TRIED TO STAY ANGRY IN THE AIR, BUT IT WAS HARD.

THE OPEN SKY INVITING ME BACK IN, AND CAROL FERRIS...

...WHY COULDN'T I STOP THINKING ABOUT HER?

CAROL,

FERRIS WANTS THIS ONE PRECISE, JORDAN. WE'RE ABOUT ROBUST TRAJECTORY TRACKING TODAY, NOT SPLIT-S MANEUVERS.

I WAS JUST LOOSENING UP.

WHAT HAPPENED TO THAT GIRL?

I DON'T KNOW IF THIS IS SUCH A GOOD IDEA, MISS FERRIS.

HE'S WANDERING ALL OVER THE PLACE. IF HE STARTS SOME OF HIS HOTDOGGING--

THIS IS HIS LAST CHANCE.

HE CAN'T SCREW IT UP.

VROOOM

WHAT IS THAT IMBECILE *DOING*?

FLYING WITHOUT HIS POWER RING.

WITHOUT HIS...? *RING*. LOCATE *HIS* POWER RING.

"THIS MAVERICK NEEDS A LESSON IN *RESPONSIBILITY*.

"BRING HIS RING TO *ME*."

WHOA!

HEY. I'VE GOT SOMETHING AT *TWELVE O'CLOCK*. THOUGHT I WAS *ALONE* UP HERE.

NOTHING ON *OUR* SCREEN. ARE YOU SURE?

VEEP VEEP VEEP

JORDAN?

COME IN, JORDAN.

BOOM

WHAT ARE YOU DOING?! *WHO* THE HELL *ARE* YOU?

I AM *SINESTRO.*

GREEN LANTERN OF *SECTOR 1417.*

IS THAT SUPPOSED TO *IMPRESS* ME?

I WOULDN'T REMEMBER UNTIL LATER, "SINESTRO" WAS ABIN SUR'S *LAST WORD.*

I NEVER THOUGHT IT WAS A NAME.

Hr.

RING?

SECTOR 1417. THE MOST ORDERLY SECTOR IN ALL THE UNIVERSE.

AND I AM THE *GREATEST* GREEN LANTERN.

WHAT THE HELL HAPPENED UP THERE?

WE DON'T KNOW, MISS FERRIS.

HE JUST *DISAPPEARED.* AND WE CAN'T MAKE *CONTACT.*

...WHO'S GOING TO SHELL OUT THE **TWENTY MILLION** DOLLARS FOR THAT JET?

I DON'T **SEE** ANY **POCKETS.**

YOUR **TERRESTRIAL AFFAIRS** SHOULD BE OF **LITTLE** CONCERN, EARTHMAN. YOU ARE IN THE PRESENCE OF A **VETERAN.**

NEVER QUESTION A **SUPERIOR OFFICER.**

NEVER CHALLENGE THOSE MORE **POWERFUL** THAN **YOU.**

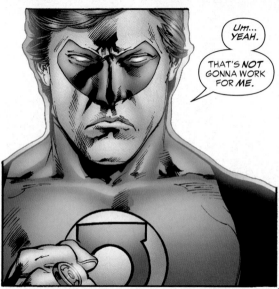

Um... **YEAH.**

THAT'S **NOT** GONNA WORK FOR **ME.**

DO YOU HAVE **ANY** IDEA WHAT YOU JUST **DID?** WHAT YOU JUST **COST** ME?

RING. CAN YOU **REBUILD** THE PLANE?

THE QUESTION SHOULDN'T BE POSED TO YOUR **RING,** IT SHOULD BE POSED TO **YOU.**

WHAT DOES **KILOWOG** TEACH YOU WHITE CIRCLES THESE DAYS?

HE TAUGHT ME THAT MY **DUTY** WAS TO LOCATE ANY **ALIENS** CAUSING **TROUBLE** AND KICK THEM **OFF** PLANET.

YOUR CONSTRUCTS ARE *WEAK*.

THEY'RE LACED WITH *ANGER*.

AND ALTHOUGH THE GUARDIANS BELIEVE *FEAR* CREATES *CRACKS* IN OUR *WILLPOWER*--

--ANGER WILL *DISTORT* IT.

ANGER WILL MAKE IT *UNFOCUSED*.

A GREEN LANTERN *NEEDS* TO BE *FOCUSED*.

OUR DUTY AS GREEN LANTERNS EXTENDS FAR BEYOND *QUELLING* ANY EXTRATERRESTRIAL CRIMES WITHIN OUR SECTOR.

THE UNIVERSE IS RAMPANT WITH *CHAOS.*

IT IS OUR DUTY TO TURN THAT CHAOS INTO *ORDER--*

--AND *MAINTAIN* IT.

HOW DID YOU...?

I NEED TO GO.

GO? GO WHERE?

BACK TO MY *REAL* JOB.

YOU NEED MORE *TRAINING*, ROOKIE.

WHAT THE HELL ARE YOU DOING HERE *ANYWAY?* TOMAR-RE TOLD ME ALL OF US ARE SUPPOSED TO STAY IN OUR *OWN* SECTOR.

YES, THE GUARDIANS' TERRITORIAL EDICT DISSUADES FRATERNIZING AMONG THE CORPS.

BUT I HAVE MY ORDERS. AND THEY ARE FROM A MUCH *HIGHER* AUTHORITY THAN TOMAR-RE.

I'VE BEEN DISPATCHED TO THIS PRIMITIVE PLANET PLAGUED WITH POLITICAL BORDERS AND TERRESTRIAL WAR TO INVESTIGATE THE DEATH OF YOUR PREDECESSOR.

ABIN SUR CRASHED HIS SHIP IN THE CALIFORNIA DESERT.

WHY?

I DON'T KNOW. HE DIDN'T TELL--

GREEN LANTERN OF SPACE SECTOR 1417--MESSAGE FROM GREEN LANTERN 2814 WAITING.

WHAT? WHAT DID YOUR RING SAY?

I DON'T KNOW. MAYBE YOURS IS SCREWING WITH IT.

MESSAGE WAITING.

STAY OUT OF MY FLIGHT PATH, SINESTRO.

I DON'T BELIEVE IT.

WHAT?

LOOK.

EEERRRTTT

OH, BOY.

WHAT THE HELL WAS *THAT?*

IT'S NOT WHAT IT LOOKS LIKE.

IT LOOKS LIKE YOU'RE PLAYING *GAMES*, MR. JORDAN.

PURPOSELY FLYING BELOW RADAR, REFUSING TO COMMUNICATE.

CAROL--

I MUST'VE BEEN *CRAZY* TO THINK THIS WAS A GOOD IDEA.

YOU'RE NOT *INSANE*, CAROL.

IN FACT, YOU HAVE QUITE A *BEAUTIFUL* MIND.

AMONG *OTHER* THINGS.

H-HECTOR?

OH MY GOD. WHAT'S HAPPENING?

WHAT'S HAPPENING? I CAN READ YOUR THOUGHTS.

DON'T *TOUCH* ME!

DON'T YOU SEE, MY DEAR, WHAT A WONDERFUL *CONNECTION* WE CAN HAVE NOW.

DEEPER THAN ANYTHING *ANYONE* HAS.

OUR MINDS WILL BE *ONE*.

AND OUR... OUR...

YOU...

HAND MORTUARY

ROOM 5

ROO

WILLIAM.

YOUR FATHER JUST FINISHED CLEANING THIS ONE UP!

I WASN'T D-D-DOING ANYTHING, MOM! I SWEAR!

HOW MANY TIMES HAVE WE TOLD YOU TO STAY *OUT* OF THE BASEMENT?

I KNOW, BUT...I JUST WANTED TO L-L-LOOK.

WHY? WHY CAN'T YOU BE A *GOOD CHRISTIAN* LIKE YOUR *BROTHERS?*

I DON'T KNOW.

YOU HAVE MET *EXTRA-TERRESTRIALS.*

LIFE FAR *BEYOND* OURS.

THEY GAVE YOU A *POWER RING.* A BAND OF *ENERGY* AND *WILL.*

THEY CALLED IT THE GREATEST *WEAPON* IN THE UNIVERSE.

THE GREATEST *TECHNOLOGY.*

HA HA HA HA HA!

GIVE ME THIS *EMERALD MIRACLE,* HAL JORDAN. GIVE...

...NO.

NO, YOU CAN'T HAVE *HER.*

NO, CAROL FERRIS IS MINE.

CHRISTINE FERRIS
Loving Wife
and Mother

SHE'S *MINE!*

I DON'T... *WANT* HER, HAMMOND.

LIAR!

KRRRAKKK*

I SEE YOUR THOUGHTS FLOATING *AROUND* YOU. EVERY LAYER OF *WHO* YOU *ARE* PEELED BACK AND ON *DISPLAY.*

I SEE THINGS NO ONE *ELSE* SEES.

YOU'VE LIVED YOUR *LIFE* TRYING TO PROVE TO EVERYONE THE *DEATH* OF YOUR FATHER DIDN'T MAKE YOU *AFRAID.*

IT'S MADE IT SO *EXCITING.*

BUT YOU HAVEN'T SHARED IT WITH *ANYONE.*

UNTIL *NOW.*

I TRIED TO POUR SOME WILL INTO THE RING, BUT IT FELT LIKE IT WAS SLIPPING OFF.

THE BEST I COULD DO —

-- WAS BLIND HIM.

AAAAaaHH!

CAROL?

H-HAL?

YOUR BOYFRIEND'S BACK.

HAL, WHAT'S GOING ON?

HE'S *NOT* MY BOYFRIEND.

LOOK AT THAT SHARED *TRAUMA.*

ALL THE *TRAGEDY* IN YOUR LIFE, IT'S NO WONDER YOU'RE *BOTH* SO *COLD.*

BUT *YOU* DON'T HAVE TO BE, CAROL. IT'S *YOUR* CHOICE.

YOU ARE ALSO BREAKING THIRTY-FOUR TERRESTRIAL AND INTERGALACTIC LAWS.

CHIEF AMONG THEM, HUMAN, IS ATTACKING AN OFFICER OF THE GREEN LANTERN CORPS.

EVEN IF I DO USE THE TERM *"OFFICER"* LOOSELY.

WHAT?

RING. *REMOVE* HIS AIR SUPPLY.

APPROXIMATELY FIVE SECONDS UNTIL THE AIR FROM HIS LUNGS IS EVACUATED.

N-NO. WHO...?

THREE.

ONE.

ASTONISHING.

A RUDIMENTARY TELEPATH LIKE THAT ACTUALLY *DISRUPTED* YOUR CONCENTRATION?

GREEN... LANTERN?

COME, ROOKIE.

WOOOSHH

...HAL?

YOU WILL CONTAIN THIS POWER OF THE BLACK FOR MY JOURNEY *HOME.*

NOW TAKE ME TO ITS HOST.

KRIK

TAKE ME TO *WILLIAM HAND.*

KRIK
KRIK
KRIK
KRIK

...*REMOVING* THE AIR FROM HIS *LUNGS* WAS A *SIMPLE* SOLUTION. WITHOUT IT, HIS TELEKINETIC BRAIN HAD NO *CHOICE* BUT TO SHUT *DOWN.*

I WOULD'VE THOUGHT OF THAT.

I DON'T THINK YOU THINK OF *ANYTHING,* JORDAN. DO YOU *EVER* PLAN AHEAD?

FOR EXAMPLE: *FLYING* TODAY.

IF I HAD NOT BROUGHT YOU YOUR RING, YOU WOULD HAVE *DIED.*

AND YOU WOULD'VE BEEN A *MURDERER. YOU* WERE THE ONE IN MY *FLIGHT PATH.*

WHY WOULD YOU EVEN FLY *WITHOUT* YOUR RING?

SOMEHOW, I DOUBT THAT.

I FORGOT IT.

FINE. LESSON *LEARNED.* CAN YOU *GO* NOW? I'VE HAD ALL THE *TRAINING* I NEED.

KILOWOG TAUGHT ME HOW TO RING SLING.

POORLY.

SALAAK HAD ME TEST THE CHARGING LIMITATIONS.

SALAAK'S *"TESTS"* ARE WORTHLESS WHEN FACED WITH THE *REALITY* OF A *"DEAD"* RING.

AND *EVERYONE* WARNED ME ABOUT THE YELLOW IMPURITY.

OF COURSE, NO ONE CAN ACTUALLY TELL ME *WHAT* THAT IS OR *WHY* IT'S THERE.

IT DOESN'T EVEN MAKE ANY SENSE.

YELLOW.

Hh.

WHAT?

I HAVE BEEN ATTEMPTING TO SEEK THE TRUTH ABOUT THE YELLOW IMPURITY FOR YEARS. I WAS SUSPENDED AFTER ACCUSING THE GUARDIANS OF PUTTING IT THERE THEMSELVES WHEN *I* WAS A ROOKIE.

DID YOU KNOW HIM?

ABIN SUR WAS *MY* MENTOR.

I SUPPOSE I QUESTIONED HIM AND DISRESPECTED HIM AS MUCH AS YOU DO ME.

HE SHOWED ME HOW TO TEMPER THAT. AND WHY IT WAS NECESSARY FOR A MEMBER OF THE GREEN LANTERN CORPS.

SO HE TOLD YOU TO SHUT UP AND PLAY GOOD SOLDIER?

OF COURSE NOT. I AM AN INDIVIDUALISTIC THINKER, AS YOU ARE. I'D NEVER BELONGED TO A GROUP LIKE THE CORPS BEFORE.

SO I HAD NEVER LEARNED HOW TO *TRUST* THE BEINGS AROUND ME.

IN PART, THAT'S WHERE MY QUESTIONING CAME FROM.

HE HELPED ME LEARN TO TRUST MY FELLOW CORPSMAN. THANKFULLY, IT DIDN'T CHANGE MY DRIVE TO SEEK THE TRUTH OR MY DETERMINATION TO ARGUE AGAINST THE THEOLOGIES I DISAGREE WITH.

THEN WHAT *DID* IT HELP YOU DO, SINESTRO?

SINESTRO. GREEN LANTERN 1417 REGISTERED IN DIRECT VICINITY. MESSAGE 22 UNLOCKED.

I REALIZE I HAVE NOT BEEN AS RIGHTEOUS AND EFFECTIVE AN OFFICER LIKE YOU OF LATE.

BUT THIS TEACHER FEARS **NOT** BEING SURPASSED BY HIS STUDENT.

YOUR **SUCCESS** IS ALL I HOPE FOR, SINESTRO.

I HAVE LEARNED THE **SECRETS** OF LIFE.

AND TO UNDERSTAND THE SEVERITY OF MY MISSION IS TO UNDERSTAND THE GREATEST **TRAGEDY** THAT HAS EVER BEFALLEN THE UNIVERSE.

A CRIME SO HORRENDOUS AND UNFATHOMABLE, IT IS **MYTH**.

LONG BEFORE THE GUARDIANS OF THE UNIVERSE RECRUITED SENTIENT LIFE FORMS INTO THE GREEN LANTERN CORPS, THEY CREATED A DIFFERENT POLICE FORCE.

ONE THEY BELIEVED WOULD NEVER BE MANIPULATED BY EMOTION. THE GUARDIANS SAW EMOTION AS A WEAKNESS IN INTELLIGENT LIFE.

THEY CONSTRUCTED THOUSANDS OF ARTIFICIAL SOLDIERS. MANHUNTERS. THEY DISPATCHED THEM ACROSS THE UNIVERSE TO MAINTAIN ORDER.

FOR EONS, THEY DID JUST THAT.

UNTIL THE MASSACRE.

"THERE WERE FIVE SURVIVORS.

"FIVE WITHIN AN ENTIRE SECTOR ONCE FULL OF LIFE."

THOSE FIVE BECAME KNOWN AS THE **FIVE INVERSIONS.** A TERRORIST CELL BENT ON THE DESTRUCTION OF THE GUARDIANS OF THE UNIVERSE.

CHIEF AMONG THEM, **ATROCITUS.**

ALONG WITH QULL, THEY SOUGHT THE **INNER POWERS** OF THE UNIVERSE. WITH THEIR RITUALS AND SACRIFICES, THEY PEERED INTO THE DEEPEST **DEPTHS** OF THE FUTURE.

AND THEY SAW **DARKNESS.**

A **BLACK** SO **DEVOID** OF LIFE, EVEN THE GUARDIANS' **LIGHT** COULD NOT PENETRATE IT.

THEY SEEK TO TAKE THIS **DARKNESS** FOR THEMSELVES AND TURN IT AGAINST US.

IT WAS FORETOLD, THAT POWER WOULD BE FOUND ON EARTH.

I KNOW YOU DO NOT BELIEVE THESE PROPHECIES, SINESTRO, NOR DO THE GUARDIANS. BUT I ASK, IN THE NAME OF OUR FRIENDSHIP, **TRUST** ME.

YOU MUST STOP THEM FROM UNLEASHING THIS DARKNESS.

IT WILL **DESTROY THE UNIVERSE.**

HE LOOKED... **SCARED--**

WHAT?

WHEN YOU SPOKE TO ABIN SUR, DID YOU SEE ANOTHER BODY?

ANOTHER **BODY,** JORDAN?

ABIN SUR WAS THE ONLY ONE I SAW IN THE SHIP. BUT HE WAS TORE UP PRETTY BAD. I THOUGHT IT WAS FROM THE CRASH. I DIDN'T THINK IT WAS BY **SOMEBODY.**

IT **WAS.**

ATROCITUS **SURVIVED.**

"WE NEED TO *FIND* HIM."

VISITING HOURS
3:30pm
5:30pm

KRIK

KRIK KRIK KRIK
KRIK KRIK KRIK

WILLIAM
HAND.

KRIK KRIK
KRIK KRIK
KRIK KRIK

YOUR INSIDES HOLD THE
DOORWAY TO ABSOLUTE
DARKNESS.

ATROCITUS!

FEEL MY *RAGE.*

KID! GET OUT OF HERE!

RUN, DAMMIT!

NNG*GF!*

WARNING. POWER LEVELS DEPLETING.

POWER LEVELS AT 38.7%

SINESTRO? WHAT'S... HAPPENING?

HE'S BUILT A COSMIC *DIVINING ROD.*

IT CAN *LOCATE* POWER--

--AND IT CAN *TAKE* IT.

WARNING. POWER LEVELS APPROACHING 0.0%

GET ON YOUR *FEET,* JORDAN.

ONE ELSE HAD TO WATCH THEIR FATHER DIE IN FRONT THEIR EYES.

THAT'S WHAT I THOUGHT MOST OF MY LIFE.

I THOUGHT I WAS ALONE.

GROWING UP, THE PILOTS WHO KNEW DAD WOULD LOOK AT ME WITH PITY WHEN I'D BEG TO GO ON A FLIGHT.

THEY ALWAYS REFUSED.

WHEN I FLEW MYSELF, THEY WOULD LOOK AT ME WITH ANNOYANCE, THINKING I WAS BREAKING THE RULES AND PUSHING THE BOUNDARIES UNTIL THE RIVETS POPPED OFF MY WINGS OUT OF ARROGANCE.

NO ONE EVER LOOKED AT ME WITH ANY KIND OF UNDERSTANDING.

NO ONE KNEW WHY I WAS THE WAY I WAS.

NOT UNTIL I MET SINESTRO.

JORDAN, FALL *BACK.*

I'VE NEVER *RUN* FROM A FIGHT BEFORE, SINESTRO. NOT GONNA START *NOW.*

YOUR RING IS *EMPTY,* LANTERN.

YOU ARE *NOTHING* TO ME.

SSLLAASSHH

GIVE ME YOUR BEST--

GET DOWN

BOOOM

IDIOT!

SPAATT

KRIK KRIK KRIK KRIK

YOU ARE STILL HERE, BOY.

DOORWAY TO THE BLACK.

WILLIAM HAND...

...YOUR INSIDES HOLD THE POWER THAT WILL DESTROY THE GUARDIANS OF THE UNIVERSE.

YOU ARE THE INCUBATOR OF DEATH TO ALL!

"FALLING BACK" IS A **MILITARY TACTIC**, JORDAN.

IT IS **NOT** A SIGN OF **FEAR**.

STANDING IN THE **LINE OF FIRE** WITH A **DRAINED** POWER RING, HOWEVER, IS A SIGN OF **STUPIDITY**.

YOU SHOULD BE **DEAD**.

YOU'RE NOT THE **FIRST** ONE TO TELL ME THAT.

I'M SHOCKED. THAT DEVICE ATROCITUS IS HOLDING IS CAPABLE OF **REMOVING** AND **CONTAINING** THE ENERGY WITHIN OUR RINGS.

WE NEED TO KEEP **CLEAR** OF IT AND WE NEED TO **RECHARGE**.

WHAT ARE YOU DOING?

RECALLING MY **POWER BATTERY**.

DON'T TELL ME SALAAK DIDN'T EDUCATE YOU ON CONFINED POCKET DIMENSIONS AND THE STORAGE OF PERSONAL CHARGING UNITS.

I KEEP MINE IN MY LOCKER.

YOU'VE REDEFINED THE WORD **CARELESS** FOR ME, JORDAN.

SO **I** TAUGHT **YOU** SOMETHING?

JUST **LIGHT UP**, ROOKIE.

HELP! SOMEBODY, PLEASE--

UnnNff!

KRRAAAATCH!

I ONLY WANTED TO... I ONLY WANTED TO SEE HOW COLD THEY WERE.

THAT'S ALL!

LEAVE ME ALONE, DEMON!

KRIK KRIK KRIK

YOUR DESTINY AWAITS.

COME **ON**, JORDAN! STOP WITH THE **HANDS** AND **FORCE SPHERES**.

OPEN UP YOUR **MIND**.

AND **STRENGTHEN** THOSE **CONSTRUCTS**.

LET **GO** OF YOUR **ANGER**!

A **ROOKIE**.

BUT **YOU**...

...I KNOW **YOU**, LANTERN.

YOU ARE **SINESTRO**.

OUR PROPHECIES SAY YOU ARE THE *GREATEST* OF THEM ALL.

THEY SAY IF *ANYONE* IS TO OPPOSE OUR *REVENGE*, IT IS *YOU.*

NM...

BUT THEY ALSO SAY YOU HAVE A *WEAKNESS.*

LIKE *ALL* OF THE GUARDIANS' TERRORISTS.

I WILL BATHE IN YOUR BLOOD, *"GREAT ONE."*

NO!

YELLOW...?

...THAT WAS...NOT POSSIBLE...

YOU KNOW MY NAME, ATROCITUS?

GOOD.

TELL THE OTHER *FOUR* OF THE *INVERSIONS* WHO THEY HAVE TO *FEAR.*

GHOOOMMM

SINESTRO. THE *GREATEST* GREEN LANTERN OF THEM *ALL.*

HEY!

HEY, KID! YOU ALL RIGHT?

HEY--!

LET THE BOY GO, JORDAN.

WHAT DID ATROCITUS WANT WITH HIM?

THEY GAIN POWER THROUGH THE BLOOD OF OTHERS THEY DEEM "DOORWAYS." BEINGS THEY BELIEVE ARE TIED TO THE GREATER FABRIC OF UNIVERSAL POWER.

UTTER NONSENSE.

YOU SAW WHAT I DID, DIDN'T YOU? WHAT DID YOU DO?

I USED THE RING AGAINST YELLOW.

YOU ASSISTED IN THIS TAKEDOWN AND ARREST, JORDAN, WITHOUT YOUR RING SEEKING A REPLACEMENT.

YOU SURVIVED. THAT'S ENOUGH.

YOU DON'T BELIEVE ME?

YOU DON'T THINK I'VE TRIED TO PIERCE THE SPECTRUM BARRIER? IT IS *FUTILE.* EVEN FOR *ME.*

I *DID.*

ENOUGH.

#$%& YOU.

UNABLE TO TRANSLATE.

HFFF. YOU HAVE TO STAND OUT, DON'T YOU?

YOU CAN'T STAND TO BE UPSTAGED?

BEING A MEMBER OF THE CORPS, YOU'LL NEED TO GET *USED* TO IT.

WHAT MAKES ANYONE THINK I *WANT* TO BE AFTER ALL THIS?

YOU NEED TO GET HOLD OF YOUR *ANGER,* JORDAN. THAT'S WHAT ALMOST GOT YOU *KILLED* TODAY.

I DON'T KNOW *WHAT* OR *WHO* YOU'RE SO *ANGRY* WITH, BUT YOU CONTINUE TO DIRECT IT AT *ME.*

YOU NEED TO *GROW UP, DEAL* WITH IT AND GET *ON* WITH YOUR *LIFE.*

YOU KNOW WHAT? I WILL.

RING. TAKE ME TO *CARL FERRIS.*

I DIDN'T LIKE SINESTRO. BUT HE WAS RIGHT. ALL THAT ANGER WASN'T ABOUT HIM.

I THOUGHT IT'D TAKE ME TO A BEACH HOUSE IN FLORIDA...

...INSTEAD I FOUND MYSELF FLYING DOWN TO HIS HOUSE OUTSIDE COAST CITY.

JORDAN? JORDAN?!

WE HAVE PROTOCOLS TO FOLLOW!

BLMMBLMM BLMM

BLMMBLMM BLMM

JORDAN?

WHAT...
...WHAT IS THIS?

HE'S SICK.

YOUR FATHER WAS HIS **BEST FRIEND.**

AND AFTER THE CRASH...

...IT **TORE** HIM UP INSIDE. AND OVER THE YEARS, THE **GUILT** TOOK ITS TOLL.

HE WAS NEVER GOLFING ON PEBBLE BEACH?

HE'S NEVER PLAYED GOLF IN HIS LIFE.

LAST YEAR, WHEN HE GOT TOO SICK TO GET OUT OF BED, FERRIS AIR WAS ALREADY IN TROUBLE.

SO YOU STOPPED FLYING? YOU STARTED RUNNING FERRIS?

AND YOU LET EVERYONE THINK YOUR FATHER WAS DOING IT ALL THROUGH **YOU?**

I DIDN'T KNOW WHAT ELSE TO DO.

THAT COMPANY. AFTER MOM AND YOUR FATHER, IT'S ALL **HE** HAD **LEFT.**

HE STILL HAS **YOU.**

I WAS A **SPOILED BRAT.**

WHEN MOM DIED, HE'D GIVE ME ANYTHING I WANTED AS LONG AS I SCREAMED **LOUD** ENOUGH.

ONE DAY, HE **REFUSED.** I DON'T EVEN KNOW WHAT I WAS AFTER, BUT I REMEMBER I SAID...

...I SAID I WISHED **MOM** WAS THERE INSTEAD OF **HIM.**

HE SAW YOU BRING YOUR DAD A BROWN BAG LUNCH AND HE TOLD ME...

...HE WISHED HE HAD A SON LIKE **YOU.**

HE WOULDN'T IF HE **KNEW** ME.

YOU'RE **HERE** FOR HIM. **ME?**

I'VE **NEVER** BEEN THERE FOR **ANYONE** IN MY FAMILY.

ALL THESE YEARS. ALL THIS *TIME*. AND I'VE *WASTED* IT.

I'VE WASTED IT *HATING* SOMEONE. BEING *ANGRY* AT SOMEONE.

SOMEONE WHO *DIDN'T* DESERVE IT.

A *LOT* OF PEOPLE WHO *DIDN'T* DESERVE IT.

I'M *SORRY*, CAROL.

I'M *SO* SORRY.

YOU'VE JUST WITNESSED THE *TRUE* POWER OF THE RING.

IT HAS HELPED YOU FIND THE *WILL* TO *LIVE.*

IT IS THE MOST *BASIC* ELEMENT WITHIN ONE'S WILLPOWER.

YOU WERE RIGHT.

I KNOW.

YOU AREN'T RIGHT ABOUT *EVERYTHING.*

BUT THE ANGER... THE ANGER I'VE HELD ONTO SINCE I WAS A *KID...*

...THAT'S BEEN FOR *NOTHING.* THAT HASN'T HELPED ANYONE.

BERATING YOU IS *MY* JOB, NOT *YOURS.*

I MYSELF HAVE SUFFERED LOSS, JORDAN. *GREAT* LOSS.

WITHOUT ABIN THERE TO HELP ME, I DOUBT THIS RING WOULD STILL BE *MINE.*

FOR BEINGS LIKE US, OVERCOMING FEAR IS WHAT WE DO BEST. BUT WHEN IT COMES TO GUILT, REGRET... *LOSS...*

...EVEN *GREEN LANTERNS* STRUGGLE WITH THOSE.

YOU ARE WELL AWARE OF THE *LIMITS* WE HAVE PUT ON THE CONGREGATION OF OUR OFFICERS *OFF* THE PLANET OA.

THESE ARE THE *GUARDIANS* OF THE *UNIVERSE?* THEY'RE SO *SMALL*--

SHUT UP.

THIS IS THE *SECOND TIME* YOU HAVE *DISOBEYED* US. AND *AGAIN* WITH THE GREEN LANTERN OF SECTOR 2814.

ALBEIT IT A *DIFFERENT* ONE. THIS IS NOT ABIN SUR.

MY NAME'S HAL JORDAN.

THEY *KNOW* THAT.

SINESTRO--?

EXPLAIN YOURSELF.

WAS SIMPLY ASSISTING THIS OFFICER IN *LOCATING* AND *ARRESTING* THE *KILLER* WHO ENDED THE LIFE OF ABIN SUR.

ATROCITUS OF THE FIVE INVERSIONS.

AND BEFORE YOU SO *ARROGANTLY* RIPPED ME AWAY FROM THAT BACKWARDS BALL OF *DIRT*, I HAD HIM IN *CUSTODY*.

WE ARE WELL *AWARE*.

ATROCITUS WAS *TETHERED* TO YOUR RING.

THIS *TERRORIST* WILL BE RETURNED TO YSMAULT WHERE HE WILL CONTINUE HIS *SENTENCE*--

--AN *ETERNITY* OF IMPRISONMENT.

HOWEVER, THIS ARREST DOES NOT EXCUSE YOU FROM BREAKING OUR TERRITORIAL EDICT, SINESTRO.

GREEN LANTERNS MUST ONLY OPERATE IN THEIR RESPECTIVE SECTORS. THEY MUST PATROL *INDEPENDENTLY*. THEY MUST FLY ON THEIR OWN--

WHY?

WORKING INDEPENDENTLY WILL MAKE YOU *STRONGER*, HAL JORDAN OF EARTH.

YOU WILL *LEARN* THAT THE ENEMIES OF *ORDER* WILL STOP AT *NOTHING* TO SPREAD *CHAOS*.

DO NOT *QUESTION* THE GUARDIANS.

WHY?

WE HAVE LIVED FOR *BILLIONS* OF YEARS.

WHAT WE DO, WE DO FOR THE *WELL-BEING* OF THE *ENTIRE* UNIVERSE.

LIKE THE *MANHUNTERS?*

JORDAN--

THE ANDROIDS THAT DID OUR JOB BEFORE THEY WENT *"GLITCHY"* AND SLAUGHTERED *EVERY* LIVING BEING IN SECTOR 666 BUT THE FIVE INVERSIONS--?

THEY ARE *LIES* FROM ATROCITUS--

IT *WASN'T* ATROCITUS THAT TOLD US ABOUT THE *MASSACRE*. IT WAS *ABIN SUR.* A MESSAGE--

MORE FABLES TO INSTILL *FEAR* AMONG YOU.

INSTILL FEAR IN *US?* YOU KNOW WHAT *I* THINK?

I THINK *YOU'RE* AFRAID.

"AND THE *BUILDINGS* ON OA, THE CITADEL OF THE GUARDIANS, THEY ALL JUST *HAPPEN* TO BE *YELLOW?*"

"BECAUSE THEY'RE *AFRAID* WE'LL TURN ON THEM LIKE THEIR *ROBOTS* DID."

THEY EXPECT *US* TO OVERCOME OUR FEARS.

WHAT ABOUT WHAT THE GUARDIANS *FEAR?*

AND THAT *TERRITORIAL EDICT?*

THAT EDICT IS $#%?!$%#.

UNABLE TO TRANSLATE.

ENOUGH. YOUR ACCUSATIONS AND DISRESPECT CAUSE US *GREAT* CONCERN.

YOU ARE ON THE VERGE OF *EXPULSION*, HAL JORDAN OF EARTH.

GUARDIANS. YOU EXPEL JORDAN, YOU CAN HAVE *MY* RING AS WELL.

OA *HELP* ME, THE EARTHMAN IS *RIGHT*.

I AM?

QUIET. *PLEASE.*

WE *CAN* BE STRONGER *TOGETHER*.

THE CORPS *SHOULD* WORK IN UNISON WHEN NECESSARY.

AND IT SHOULD BE UP TO *US* TO NOT ONLY HELP OUR FELLOW OFFICERS *GROW*, BUT TO KEEP THEM IN *CHECK*. TO INSURE THAT THE TRAGEDY THAT HAPPENED IN SECTOR 666 *NEVER* HAPPENS AGAIN.

ALL OF *THIS*. THIS STARTED BECAUSE ONE OF YOU *SENT* ME TO ASSIST ABIN SUR'S REPLACEMENT.

ONE OF US?

THE ONE WHO CALLS HIMSELF "*GANTHET*."

"GANTHET"?
WE TAKE **NO** NAMES.
ONE OF YOU **HAS**.

WHICH ONE?

I BELIEVE WE HAVE HEARD **MUCH** TO CONSIDER, SINESTRO. FOR NOW, WE LEAVE THE EARTHMAN WITH HIS RING.
AND OBVIOUSLY, **YOU** WITH **YOURS**.

YES. BUT HE IS NOW AS MUCH **YOUR** RESPONSIBILITY AS KORUGAR AND THE REST OF SECTOR 1417.

WE **TRUST** THAT IS **ACCEPTABLE**, SINESTRO...
...**GREATEST** OF THE **GREEN** LANTERNS.

Hr.
YES.

"THAT IS ACCEPTABLE."

HNNN!!

FSSSSS

I DID DO IT.

YOU DIDN'T DO IT.

I DID.

NO ONE CAN BREAK THROUGH YELLOW, JORDAN. NOT EVEN SINESTRO.

I CAN--

YOU ONLY TRIED LIKE TWENTY TIMES, HUMAN! YOU CAN TRY ANOTHER THOUSAND AND IT WON'T MAKE A DIFFERENCE.

I BELIEVE HIM.

YOU, TOMAR-RE? YOU ALWAYS HAD FAITH FAR TOO READILY.

I SUPPOSE THAT IS ONE THING ABIN TAUGHT ME THAT HE NEVER TAUGHT YOU.

I SUPPOSE...

...I MUST GO.

I DO NOT HAVE TIME FOR ANY MORE GAMES...

...THE GUARDIANS HAVE BOTHERED ME WITH THE *TASK* OF RETURNING ATROCITUS TO YSMAULT.

SINESTRO.

IF YOU'RE GOING TO SAY ANYTHING, JORDAN, SAY "I WON'T MAKE YOU *REGRET* THIS."

I WON'T.

THAT IS ALL I NEED TO HEAR, BECAUSE, *UNFORTUNATELY*, A "GOODBYE" IS NOT APPROPRIATE.

WE WILL RECONVENE IN ONE MONTH SO THAT I MAY EVALUATE YOUR PROGRESS.

BUT *NEXT* TIME--

--YOU'RE COMING TO *MY* WORLD.

I GUESS NOT.

BUT BEING THE ONLY PILOT--

FOR NOW.

BEING THE ONLY PILOT, YOU'RE GOING TO BE LOGGING A HELLUVA LOT OF *FLIGHT TIME.*

THAT'S WHAT I'M HOPING.

I STILL DON'T GET WHY YOU WANT TO FLY A *PLANE* WHEN YOU'VE GOT THAT *MAGIC RING.*

THE RING'S NOT *MAGIC.* THE PLANES ARE.

SPEAKING OF. WHICH ONE AM I TAKING UP TODAY?

THAT ONE OVER THERE.

FWUMP

THIS IS... THIS IS THAT HUNK OF JUNK. THIS IS THE PLANE MY DAD FLEW ME IN. BUT--

I'M GOOD, *huh?* ONLY TOOK ME THREE WEEKS.

IT'S AMAZING, TOM.

IT SEEMED LIKE SHE MEANT A LOT TO YOU. I TOLD MISS FERRIS. SHE SAID I COULD FIX IT UP.

CAROL DID?

WHEN EVERY OTHER PILOT *LEFT*, I NEEDED *SOMETHING* TO KEEP YOU HERE.

BUT IT'S *MISS FERRIS,* JORDAN. NOT "*CAROL.*"

WHAT ARE YOU STARING AT?

HOPEFULLY, THE GIRL I'M HAVING DINNER WITH TONIGHT.

OH, JORDAN. *EVERYONE* KNOWS--

--I DON'T *DATE* EMPLOYEES.

GET IN THE AIR.

RIGHT AWAY, MISS FERRIS.

EDWARDS AIR FORCE BASE. HANGAR 44.

ANYTHING SPECIAL PLANNED TONIGHT?

HEADING DOWN TO PANCHO'S WITH THE GUYS. MY GIRLFRIEND'S BEEN A PAIN LATELY. SHE'S BEEN ON MY CASE ABOUT THE "NEXT LEVEL" OF OUR RELATIONSHIP.

I TOLD HER THE NEXT LEVEL IS ME MOVIN' ON OUT!

I HAVE A GIRLFRIEND TOO.

DO YOU HEAR ME?

HELLO?

ANYONE? DO YOU HEAR ME?

YOU CAN'T LEAVE ME IN HERE. THIS IS A TERRIBLY EMPTY PLACE! A VILE PLACE!

I'M NOT LIKE THAT ALIEN SHIP! I'M NOT HERE TO BE POKED AND PRODDED!

DON'T LISTEN TO THE GREEN LANTERN!

HE IS AMAZING THOUGH. THE LIFE HE LIVES IS SO THRILLING.

THE LEAPS AND THE FLIGHTS AND THE WOMEN.

THE WOMEN.

I WANT TO BE A PART OF THAT EXCITEMENT. OH, IT'LL BE WONDERFUL WHEN I AM AGAIN!

YES, OH, YES!

I'M FEELING BETTER ALREADY.

...REPORTS OF MORE **STRANGE LIGHTS** IN THE SKY ARE POURING IN.

COAST CITY HOSPITAL CCH

U.F.O.'S? SECRET AIR FORCE TEST FLIGHTS? OR ARE THESE RUMORS OF A GLOWING GREEN **MAN** TRUE?

IS THE **GREEN LANTERN** REAL?

WITH THE RECENT APPEARANCE OF **SUPERMAN** IN METROPOLIS, COULD COAST CITY HAVE ITS VERY OWN PROTECTOR? AN EMERALD WARRIOR--?

KLANK

KLK

CHRIST.

I D-D-DIDN'T DO ANYTHING **WRONG.**

STAND **UP.** STAND UP AND GET AWAY FROM THAT--

SWAAEE!

FWAAKSSH

IT'S OKAY. DEAD IS G-G-GOOD.

DEAD IS **GOOD.**

YSMAULT.

BY ORDER OF THE GUARDIANS, I RETURN YOU TO YOUR CRUCIFIX, ATROCITUS.

YOU ARE TO SERVE OUT THE REMAINDER OF YOUR SENTENCE FOR YOUR CRIMES.

NNYYAAA!

FAREWELL, FELON.

WE WITNESSED THE FATE OF ABIN SUR, SINESTRO!

WE CAN SEE ANOTHER!

YOUR TALES WILL NOT FRIGHTEN ME, QULL. I CAN LOOK OUT FOR MYSELF.

QULL IS NOT SPEAKING OF YOU, SINESTRO. I SEE IT NOW TOO.

AS DO I.

KORUGAR.

YOUR HOMEWORLD WILL SOON DESCEND INTO CIVIL *UNREST.* *VIOLENT* RIOTS. A *BLOODY* COUP.

YOUR PEOPLE WILL PLUNGE INTO *MADNESS* AS YOU SAVE WORLDS *NOT* YOUR OWN.

CHAOS WILL SPIN IT OUT OF YOUR *CONTROL.*

YOU THINK ME A *FOOL,* ATROCITUS?

KORUGAR WILL *NEVER* EMBRACE *CHAOS.* NOT AS LONG AS I AM AROUND TO INSTILL *ORDER.*

I FEEL *NO FEAR,* DEMONS.

NO FEAR OF *ANY* KIND.

THEN ONE DAY, YOU WILL FEEL MY *RAGE,* GREEN LANTERN.

AND YOU WILL *BURN* BY IT.

HAL?

JACK'S NOT COMING.

I'M SORRY.

JIM?

I DIDN'T THINK HE WOULD.

I DON'T *BLAME* HIM. I WOULDN'T HAVE BLAMED YOU *EITHER*.

I'VE *NEVER* BEEN A GOOD *BROTHER*.

THE END

GEOFF JOHNS is one of the most prolific and popular contemporary comic book writers. He has written highly acclaimed stories starring Superman, Green Lantern, the Flash, Teen Titans, and Justice Society of America. He is the author of *The New York Times* best-selling graphic novels GREEN LANTERN: RAGE OF THE RED LANTERNS, GREEN LANTERN: SINESTRO CORPS WAR, JUSTICE SOCIETY OF AMERICA: THY KINGDOM COME, SUPERMAN: BRAINIAC and BLACKEST NIGHT.

Johns was born in Detroit and studied media arts, screenwriting, film production and film theory at Michigan State University. After moving to Los Angeles, he worked as an intern and later an assistant for film director Richard Donner, whose credits include *Superman: The Movie, Lethal Weapon 4* and *Conspiracy Theory*.

Johns began his comics career writing STARS AND S.T.R.I.P.E. and creating Stargirl for DC Comics. He received the Wizard Fan Award for Breakout Talent of 2002 and Writer of the Year for 2005, 2006, 2007 and 2008 as well as the CBG Writer of the Year 2003 through 2005 and 2007 and 2008, and CBG Best Comic Book Series for JSA 2001 through 2005.

After acclaimed runs on THE FLASH, TEEN TITANS and the best-selling INFINITE CRISIS miniseries, Johns co-wrote a run on ACTION COMICS with his mentor Donner. In 2006, he co-wrote 52: an ambitious weekly comic book series set in real time, with Grant Morrison, Greg Rucka and Mark Waid. Johns has also written for various other media, including the acclaimed "Legion" episode of SMALLVILLE and the fourth season of ROBOT CHICKEN. He wrote the story of the DC Universe Online massively multiplayer action game from Sony Online Entertainment LLC and has recently joined DC Entertainment as its Chief Creative Officer.

Johns currently resides in Los Angeles, California.

IVAN REIS is a comic book artist born in 1976 in São Bernardo do Campo, São Paulo, Brazil. He started his US career in the '90s, on *Ghost* and *The Mask* for Dark Horse. After pencilling an issue of THE INVISIBLES for Grant Morrison, he started a long run on *Lady Death* for Chaos Comics, then did *The Avengers* and *The Vision*, with Geoff Johns, for Marvel. In 2004 Ivan began to work exclusively for DC. After illustrating high-profile series such as ACTION COMICS, INFINITE CRISIS and RANN-THANAGAR WAR, he started his now legendary run on GREEN LANTERN and BLACKEST NIGHT with Geoff Johns, and continues his association with Geoff on BRIGHTEST DAY.

Never let fear overcome you.

Since we reintroduced Hal Jordan and the Green Lantern Corps in 2004's GREEN LANTERN: REBIRTH, fear has been at the center of our stories. In our world, fear is a force in our lives that we can't touch or quantify, but it is very real. It's something that can keep us from following our dreams, it can create hate and it can paralyze us from living our lives with the freedom we all deserve. I wanted to make fear very real in the world of GREEN LANTERN, and I think that's part of the success of the characters. It's not that Green Lanterns are chosen because they have no fear, it's because they have the ability to overcome fear.

But not everyone does.

Some people give in to fear and live a life surrounded by it. This is exactly what happens to Doctor Hector Hammond in the upcoming GREEN LANTERN film. But before I briefly talk about Hector Hammond, let me back up and acknowledge that bizarrely cool still up there.

If you're reading this, chances are you already know that 2011 summer sees the release of the first-ever live-action GREEN LANTERN movie starring Ryan Reynolds as the quintessential Hal Jordan, the wonderful Blake Lively as Carol Ferris, Mark Strong as the perfect Sinestro and the unbelievable Peter Sarsgaard as Hector Hammond. If you didn't know we're that close to seeing Kilowog, Oa, Ferris Air and the Guardians of the Universe up on the big screen, now you do.

Last summer, I was on set down in smoldering New Orleans with producer Donald De Line during one of the scenes with Hal and Hector. (And to give you an idea of how into it Donald is, he was wearing his Green Lantern ring.) When Peter Sarsgaard walked on stage in full makeup it was scary. Hector Hammond has been a longtime character in the comics, someone I've enjoyed writing myself, but this scientist turned highly evolved telepath was never portrayed as frightening or as human as this. I was captivated watching director Martin Campbell (*Casino Royale, The Mask of Zorro*) work with Peter on getting a performance that, for me, elevated Hector Hammond to an entirely new level. Peter took the air out of the room. We were all speechless, mesmerized not only by the makeup that turned this grotesque longtime enemy of Green Lantern into a reality, but more important, by each and every word coming out of Peter's mouth. Hector Hammond has become a formidable and very real force for fear.

Coming up you'll get looks at Hal's power battery and ring, the aliens of the Green Lantern Corps, Oa, the Guardians of the Universe and even the greatest Green Lantern that's ever lived… Sinestro!

All will be well,

Geoff Johns

GREEN LANTERN

EXCLUSIVE MOVIE PREVIEW

In the film Peter Sarsgaard

Mark Strong IS Sinestro!

THE GREATEST GREEN LANTERN!

Before Sinestro fell from grace, becoming the ultimate Green Lantern villain and one of the greatest foes in history… he was the finest Green Lantern ever.

Respected by his Corpsmen and trusted by the immortal Guardians of the Universe, Sinestro is considered the greatest Green Lantern, having preserved definitive order in his sector. This regal Korugarian commands attention and needed an actor that could portray the same. Could anyone live up to the perfection of Sinestro?

Have No Fear, for Mark Strong IS Sinestro!

When Mark Strong *(Sherlock Holmes, Robin Hood, Kick Ass)* arrived on the set decked out in make-up and prosthetics, I thought Sinestro had walked right off the comics page. Take a look at that still… just incredible!

Back in August, I visited the Green Lantern movie set with Blackest Night and Sinestro Corps masterminds Geoff Johns and Ivan Reis – and what a trip it was. My mind is still blown from the experience. I was given the opportunity to hold the actual Power Battery and was able to wear the Green Lantern ring… *In Brightest Day, In Blackest –* sorry, got carried away. I could go on for pages about the amazing production designs, how surreal Ryan Reynolds looked in Hal Jordan's flight suit, or how awestruck I was by early CG tests of Oa and the different alien Green Lanterns, but instead let me focus on the supreme highlight.

Sinestro.

I witnessed scenes of Sinestro in action, addressing the entire Corps, and speaking with the Guardians. The entire time I was glued to my seat, unable to turn away. Mark nailed it all. The voice – the demeanor – everything! Mark, like much of the film, has taken his inspiration from Geoff Johns's extraordinary run on GREEN LANTERN.

The same care and enthusiasm is being brought to the Green Lantern movie by visionary director Martin Campbell *(Casino Royale)*, producer Donald De Line and the rest of the cast and crew. I am beyond excited and can't wait for them to introduce the Green Lantern universe to millions. It will be the year of Green Lantern.

Long Live the Corps!!!!

Adam Schlagman
(Green Lantern Editor)

IT'S ALL IN THE DETAILS…

…is a mantra Tomar-Re lives by which has aided him in becoming an honored and highly respected Green Lantern. It's also a mantra that the filmmakers, like production designer Grant Major, costume designer Ngila Dickson and visual effects supervisor Jim Berny have taken as their own. Producer Donald De Line and director Martin Campbell have assembled an amazing corps.

Growing up on the planet Xudar, Tomar-Re comes from a peaceful avian race that focuses their efforts on the arts and sciences instead of war. His nature to examine everything has led the Guardians of the Universe to appoint him the archivist and protector of the sacred Book of Oa. When not studying the nature of the Corps, Tomar-Re patrols sector 2813 where he developed a close friendship with neighboring sector 2814's Green Lantern, Abin Sur. Tomar has taken an interest in Abin's replacement Hal Jordan. Though Hal is *not* one for details, Tomar hopes to teach Hal what it means to be a Green Lantern.

Now the same thoughtfulness that Tomar-Re believes in is being utilized to bring him and the rest of the Green Lantern Corps to life on the big screen.

We've watched test after test supervised by digital effects master Jim Berney based on the amazing design work by Grant and Ngila. Their passion for detail is much like Tomar-Re's. Something I found extremely interesting was the mix of motion capture and straight-up animation they used in creating the Green Lantern Corps. Some of the more humanoid Corps members like Tomar-Re and Kilowog started with motion capture, but most of their flying and movement beyond simple interaction was animated, some based on the movement of insects or animals and others created completely from scratch – giving them all a unique, and alien, feel. It's this attention to detail – from the scales on Tomar-Re's skin to the way he turns when he flies into the air – that will give the Green Lantern Corps more life than it's ever seen.

With talented people like Grant, Ngila and Jim and his team pouring their heart and soul into this, it makes you realize even more than you might already how truly amazing the Green Lantern universe is.

Let's follow the advice that Tomar-Re would give to Hal: Follow your heart, believe in your will and never, ever disrespect Sinestro!

Geoff Johns

EXCLUSIVE
MOVIE
PREVIEW

Tomar-Re brought to life by Sony Imageworks.

KILOWOG - as brought to life by Sony Imageworks

EXCLUSIVE MOVIE PREVIEW

GREEN LANTERN

One of the greatest challenges for the upcoming Green Lantern film is bringing the Green Lantern Corps to life. It falls to the work of dozens of people overseen by director Martin Campbell and led by production designer Grant Major and costume designer Ngila Dickson.

We've taken a look at the spiritual trainer of the Corps in previous issues with Tomar-Re, but this time the big guy takes the stage. Perhaps the most popular alien Green Lantern – next to Sinestro, of course – is the one member of the Green Lantern Corps that can whip any rookie Lantern into shape. Even an Earthman named Hal Jordan.

If the saying "Beware my power" were true for any other Corps member, it'd be the Green Lantern known as KILOWOG.

Along with every other GL fan, my introduction to this brute of a GL was in 1986's *Green Lantern Corps* #201. Kilowog looked among the most alien of the existing GLs of the day. The lone survivor of his home world Bolovax Vik, he came from a society of decidedly Socialist views—ideal for a police force where there is no rank. Now, of course, he spends most of his time on the Corps' headquartered world of Oa.

And yet, his tough exterior and demeanor belies a thoughtful soul, and one couldn't ask for a better ally in letting no evil escape your sight. Kilowog might be tough as a rhino on his trainees, doing anything he can to motivate and educate them. Without a family to call his own, he embraces his rookies as if they were, with a tough love designed to keep them alive and do right by the ideals of the Corps.

The filmmakers have captured the essence of Kilowog perfectly in the film. And with film, there's an entirely new dimension to Kilowog and the rest of the Corps members. You'll see them brought to life with detail and power you could never imagine.

Beware his power!

Brian Cunningham
Green Lantern Editor